Float or Sink?

HEINLE
CENGAGE Learning

Young & Son
Global, Inc.

Which of your toys float?

Contents

float

sink

ball

rock

toy car

apple

Some things float.
Some things sink.

Look at this ball.
Will this ball float?

Yes. This ball floats.

Look at this rock.
Will this rock float?

No. This rock does not float.
It sinks.

Look at this toy car.
Will this toy car sink?

Yes. This toy car sinks.

Will this apple float?

Do these things float or sink?

What Floats or Sinks?

Some things float and some things sink.
What will float? What will sink?
Look at this ball. It will float.
Look at this rock. It will sink.
Some things float and some things sink.
Now I know what floats or sinks.

Index